THE UNOFFICIAL GUIDE

Contents

INTRODUCTION

Greetings and welcome to this comprehensive, unofficial handbook dedicated to the Paris Olympics 2024. Within the pages of this guide, you will find detailed insights into the eagerly awaited opening ceremony, the exciting array of sporting competitions comprising the games, and the noteworthy events that coalesce to elevate this global athletic extravaganza to unparalleled significance.

Embark on a journey through the enchanting world of the Paris Olympics as we delve into the intricacies of the grand opening ceremony, a spectacle set to captivate audiences worldwide with its grandeur and artistic prowess. Explore the games themselves, each contest symbolizing the pinnacle of athletic prowess and sporting excellence, with detailed guides providing an immersive experience into the heart of the competition.

Discover the events that collectively contribute to the Paris Olympics' status as the foremost international sporting spectacle. From thrilling competitions to cultural showcases, this guide aims to encapsulate the essence of an event that stands as a beacon of unity and competition on the global stage.

In addition to the Olympic fervor, this guide extends its reach to the vibrant city of Paris, offering insights into the people, places, and cultural marvels that make the host city a focal point of attention during this momentous occasion. Navigate through the thorough listings of events, ensuring you don't miss a moment of the action, and delve into a comprehensive breakdown of the countries participating, highlighting the diverse array of nations converging to celebrate the spirit of sportsmanship and camaraderie.

This unofficial guide serves as your passport to the Paris Olympics 2024, providing an extensive and immersive experience that goes beyond the stadiums and ceremonies, offering a holistic view of the people, places, and events that collectively shape this global celebration of athleticism.

THE OLYMPIC SYMBOL

THE UNOFFICIAL
GUIDE

PARiS 2024

The emblem for Paris 2024 ingeniously intertwines three distinct symbols – the gold medal, the flame, and Marianne, the embodiment of the French Republic. Each of these symbols has been carefully chosen to encapsulate various facets of our identity and values. Notably, this emblem marks a historic moment as it is the first time a singular emblem has been designated for both the Olympic Games and the Paralympic Games.

THE GOLD MEDAL – A Testament to Achievement

The gold medal stands as a testament to the remarkable achievements of our Olympic and Paralympic athletes, revered as the true heroes of the Games. Their dedication is exemplified through exceeding personal bests, showcasing that the spirit of victory is accessible to everyone. We recall iconic moments such as Renaud Lavillenie's triumphant last attempt at securing the Olympic title in London and Marie Amélie Le Fur's awe-inspiring three gold medals and two world records at the Paralympic Games in Rio.

Yet, the significance of the Paris 2024 Games' medal extends beyond champions; it is a token of appreciation for all those who give their all, fostering an environment where others can do the same.

THE FLAME – Shared Energy Incarnate

The Olympic and Paralympic flame bears a potent message, evoking varied meanings and emotions among different individuals. Memorable instances include Cathy Freeman, the Indigenous athlete chosen for the anchor leg in the relay at Sydney in 2000, and Paralympic Archer Antonio Rebollo, who ignited the torch by skillfully firing an arrow in Barcelona in 1992.

The flame symbolizes the unique energy propelling this colossal event, inspiring us to be daring and innovate in organizing the Games, addressing the contemporary challenges that confront us.

MARIANNE – The Essence of France

Marianne embodies the bold spirit of creativity, symbolizing the inspiration behind our Games. As the personification of the French Republic, Marianne represents values harmonious with those found in sport, the Olympics, and the Paralympics – humanism, fraternity, generosity, and sharing. A familiar presence in French culture, Marianne graces stamps and adorns town halls, reflecting our commitment to organizing the Games for the people, in collaborative harmony with the populace.

THE OPENING CEREMONY

Departing from historical norms, the opening ceremony of the Paris 2024 Olympics promises to be a groundbreaking and distinctive spectacle, destined to etch its place among the most memorable moments in the Olympic chronicles. This momentous occasion is set to introduce several unprecedented features that will redefine the traditional Olympic inauguration.

One of the most notable departures from convention is the decision to break free from the confines of a stadium. For the first time in the annals of the Summer Olympic Games, the opening ceremony will unfold beyond the stadium walls, taking to the vibrant streets of Paris. The heart of the city, along the iconic Seine River, will serve as the unconventional stage for this extraordinary event. The parade of athletes, a hallmark of Olympic ceremonies, will undergo a transformation as it navigates the Seine, with each national delegation showcased on boats equipped with cameras. This innovative approach aims to bring the athletes closer to the audience, offering television and online viewers an intimate perspective on the participants as they traverse the city from east to west. The 6 km route will culminate in front of the Trocadéro, where the final elements of the Olympic protocol and captivating shows will unfold.

In a move that further amplifies the inclusivity of this groundbreaking ceremony, a considerable portion of the spectators will enjoy the festivities without the need for admission tickets. The upper quays will be open to the public, ensuring that hundreds of thousands of spectators can partake in the celebration along the banks of the Seine. For those seeking a more immersive experience on the lower quays, extending from the Austerlitz bridge to the Iéna bridge, tickets will be available for purchase. The decision to make this ceremony accessible to a vast audience, free of charge for many, is a pioneering approach, making it the largest opening ceremony in the history of the Games.

Central to the uniqueness of the Paris 2024 opening ceremony is its deliberate focus on athletes. The parade of delegations, an iconic element, will place athletes at the forefront, a departure from tradition. Throughout the ceremony, athletes will share the stage with performers, embodying Paris 2024's commitment to creating an Olympic experience tailored for and shaped by the athletes themselves. This emphasis on the sporting protagonists from the very beginning underscores the event's dedication to honouring the spirit and essence of the Games. As Paris opens its arms to the world, both local residents and global visitors are invited to partake in this unparalleled celebration of athleticism and unity.

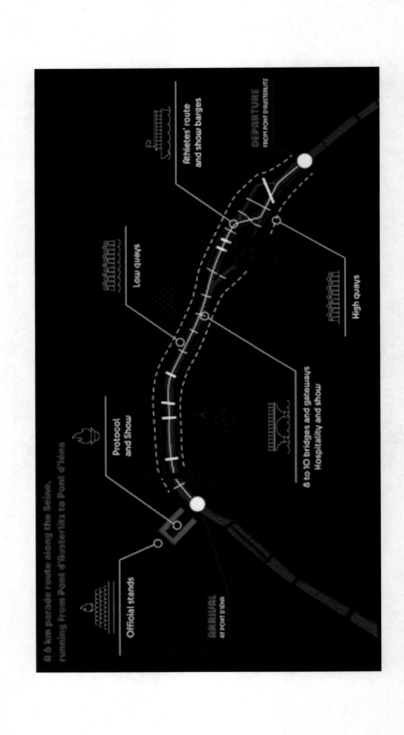

Paris 2024 Sports

Here is an alphabetical list of all of the sports in the Paris 2024 Olympic Games in alphabetical order.

3x3 Basketball Archery Artistic Gymnastics Artistic Swimming Athletics Badminton Basketball Beach Volleyball Boxing Breaking Canoe Sprint Canoe Slalom Cycling BMX Freestyle Cycling BMX Racing Cycling Mountain Bike Cycling Road Cycling Track Diving Equestrian Fencing Football Golf Handball Hockey Judo Marathon Swimming Modern Pentathlon Rhythmic Gymnastics Rowing Rugby Sevens Sailing Shooting Skateboarding Sport Climbing Surfing Swimming Table Tennis Taekwondo Tennis Trampoline Triathlon Volleyball Water Polo Weightlifting Wrestling

Breaking will make its Olympic debut in Paris.

3 recently introduced Olympics sports will return: Surfing, skateboarding and climbing.

Karate has been dropped as an Olympic sport.

FULL EVENTS LIST

Seeking details about when your favorite sport or desired event takes place at the Olympic Games Paris 2024? Look no further; we have you covered.

The Organising Committee initially revealed the competition session schedule, sport by sport, last July, marking the two-year countdown to the Games.

A noteworthy deviation from previous Olympic Games is the extension of an additional day to the swimming schedule. This adjustment translates to thrilling action in athletics, artistic gymnastics, and swimming – three of the most eagerly anticipated sports globally – occurring simultaneously on both 3 and 4 August 2024.

Explore the day-by-day guide outlining all 329 medal events below. It's crucial to note that the schedule information presented here is preliminary and not definitive; alterations to the competition schedule may occur until the conclusion of the Olympic Games Paris 2024. The latest update was on 2 April 2023.

All specified times are in Paris time (Central European Summer Time), unless otherwise indicated.

CEST is 1 hour ahead of British Summer Time, 2 hours ahead of UTC, 6 hours ahead of North American Eastern Daylight Time, and 9 hours ahead of North American Pacific Daylight Time. Additionally, it is 3 hours 30 minutes behind India Standard Time, 8 hours behind Australian Eastern Standard Time, and 10 hours behind New Zealand Standard Time.

Wednesday 24 July 2024

These events take place BEFORE the opening ceremony on Friday.
- Football: 1500-2300: M group stage (8 matches)

- Rugby sevens: 1530-2200: M pool rounds

Thursday 25 July 2024

These events take place BEFORE the opening ceremony on Friday.

- Archery: 0930-1230: W ranking round; 1415-1715: M ranking round

- Football: 1700-2300: W group stage (6 matches)

- Handball: 0900-1230: W preliminaries (2 matches); 1400-1730: W preliminaries (2 matches); 1900-2230: W preliminaries (2 matches)

- Rugby sevens: 1400-1700: M pool rounds; 2000-2300: M placement matches, quarters

Friday 26 July 2024

Friday 26th July is dominated by the opening cermony on the Seine.

Saturday 27 July 2024 (14 gold medal events)

- Artistic gymnastics: 1100-1330; 1530-1800; 2000-2230: M qualifications

- Badminton: 0830-1200: M/W/Mixed singles & doubles group stage; 1400-1730: M/W/Mixed singles & doubles group stage; 1930-2300: M/W singles & doubles group stage

- Basketball: 1100-1515: M group phase (2 matches); 1715-1900: M group phase (1 match); 2100-2245: M group phase (1 match)

- Beach volleyball: 1400-1600: M/W preliminary phase (2 matches); 1800-2000: M/W preliminary phase (2 matches); 2200-0000: M/W preliminary phase (2 matches)

- Boxing: 1530-1755: W 54kg, W 60kg, M 63.5kg, M 80kg round of 32 or round of 16; 2000-2255: W 54kg, W 60kg, M 63.5kg, M 80kg round of 32 or round of 16

- Canoe slalom: 1500-1910: M C1 heats, W K1 heats

- Diving: **1100-1200: W synchro 3m springboard final**

- Equestrian: 0930-1830: Eventing dressage

- Fencing: 1000-1640: W épée, M sabre through quarters; **1900-2250: W épée, M sabre semis, medal finals**

- Football: 1500-2300: M group stage (8 matches)

- Handball: 0900-1230: M preliminaries (2 matches); 1400-1730: M preliminaries (2 matches); 1900-2230: M preliminaries (2 matches)

- Hockey: 1000-1500: M pool stage (2 matches); 1030-1530: M pool stage (2 matches); 1700-2200: M/W pool stage (2 matches); 1730-2230: M/W pool stage (2 matches)

- Judo: 1000-1400: W -48kg, M -60kg elimination rounds; **1600-1900: W -48kg, M -60kg medal rounds**

- Road cycling: **1430-1830: M/W ind. time trial finals**

- Rowing: 0900-1310: M single sculls, W single sculls, M double sculls, W double sculls, M quadruple sculls, W quadruple sculls heats

- Rugby sevens: **1430-2045: M placement matches, semis, medal finals**

- Shooting: 0900-1345: M/W 10m air pistol, Mixed team 10m air rifle qualification; **1030-1150: Mixed team 10m air rifle finals**

- Skateboard: 1200-1530: M street preliminaries; **1700-1900: M street medal final**

- Surfing: 1900-0430 (0700-1630 Tahiti time): M/W round 1

- Swimming: 1100-1300: W 100m fly, W 400m free, M 100m breast, M 400m free, W 4x100m free relay, M 4x100m free relay heats; **2030-2230: W 100m fly semis, M 400m free, W 400m free finals**, M 100m breast semis, **W 4x100m free relay, M 4x100m free relay finals**

- Table tennis: 1500-1800: M/W singles preliminary round, Mixed doubles round of 16; 2000-2300: M/W singles round 1

- Tennis: 1200-1700 (Court Philippe Chartrier): M/W singles; 1900-2300 (Court Philippe Chartrier): M/W singles; 1200-1900 (Court Suzanne Lenglen): M/W singles, doubles; 1200-1900 (Court Simonne Mathieu): M/W singles, doubles; 1200-1900 (outside courts): M/W singles, doubles

- Volleyball: 0900-1130: M preliminary round; 1300-1530: M preliminary round; 1700-1930: M preliminary round; 2100-2330: M preliminary round

- Water polo: 1400-1700: W preliminary round (2 matches); 1830-2130: W preliminary round (2 matches)

Sunday 28 July 2024 (13 gold medal events)

- Archery: 0930-1105: W team eliminations; **1415-1755: W team medal rounds**

- Artistic gymnastics: 0930-1320; 1450-1630; 1800-1940; 2110-2250: W qualifications

- Badminton: 0830-1200: M/W/Mixed singles & doubles group stage; 1400-1730: M/W/Mixed singles & doubles group stage; 1930-2300: M/W/Mixed singles & doubles group stage

- Basketball: 1100-1515: M/W group phase (2 matches); 1715-1900: M/W group phase (1 match); 2100-2245: M/W group phase (1 match)

- Beach volleyball: 0900-1300: M/W preliminary phase (4 matches); 1500-1800: M/W preliminary phase (3 matches); 2000-2300: M/W preliminary phase (3 matches)

- Boxing: 1100-1310: W 50kg, W 66kg, M 51kg, M 57kg, M 71kg, M 92kg round of 32 or round of 16; 1530-1740: W 50kg, W 66kg, M 51kg, M 57kg, M 71kg, M 92kg round of 32 or round of 16; 2000-2210: W 50kg, W 75kg, M 71kg, M 92kg round of 32 or round of 16

- Canoe slalom: **1530-1850: W K1 semis, finals**

- Equestrian: 1030-1500: Eventing cross-country

- Fencing: 0930-1650: M épée, W foil through quarters; **1900-2310: M épée, W foil semis, medal finals**

- Football: 1700-2300: W group stage (6 matches)

- Handball: 0900-1230: W preliminaries (2 matches); 1400-1730: W preliminaries (2 matches); 1900-2230: W preliminaries (2 matches)

- Hockey: 1000-1500: W pool stage (2 matches); 1030-1530: W pool stage (2 matches); 1700-2200: M pool stage (2 matches); 1730-2230

- Judo: 1000-1400: W -52kg, M -66kg elimination rounds; **1600-1900: W -52kg, M -66kg medal rounds**

- Mountain bike: **1400-1630: W cross-country final**

- Rowing: 0900-1310: W single sculls, M single sculls, W double sculls, M double sculls repechage, W coxless pair, M coxless pair, W lightweight double sculls, M lightweight double sculls, W coxless four, M coxless four heats

- Rugby sevens: 1530-2200: W pool rounds

- Sailing: 1100-1900: M/W windsurfing, skiff

- Shooting: 0915-1230: M/W 10m air rifle qualification; **0930-1305: M/W 10m air pistol finals**

- Skateboard: 1200-1530: W street preliminaries; **1700-1900: W street medal final**

- Surfing: 1900-0430 (0700-1630 Tahiti time): M/W round 2

- Swimming: 1100-1300: M 200m free, M 400m IM, W 100m breast, M 100m back, W 200m free heats; **2030-2230: M 400m IM, W 100m fly finals**, M 200m free, W 100m breast, M 100m back semis, **M 100m breast final**, W 200m free semis

- Table tennis: 1000-1400: M/W singles round 1; 1600-1800: Mixed doubles quarters; 2000-2300: M/W singles round 1

- Tennis: 1200-1700 (Court Philippe Chartrier): M/W singles; 1900-2300 (Court Philippe Chartrier): M/W singles; 1200-1900 (Court Suzanne Lenglen): M/W singles, doubles; 1200-1900 (Court Simonne Mathieu): M/W singles, doubles; 1200-1900 (outside courts): M/W singles, doubles

- Volleyball: 0900-1130: W preliminary round; 1300-1530: W preliminary round; 1700-1930: M preliminary round; 2100-2330: M preliminary round

- Water polo: 1030-1330: M preliminary round (2 matches); 1500-1800: M preliminary round (2 matches); 1930-2230: M preliminary round (2 matches)

Monday 29 July 2024 (18 gold medal events)

- Archery: 0930-1105: M team eliminations; **1415-1755: M team medal rounds**

- Artistic gymnastics: **1730-2030: M team final**

- Badminton: 0830-1200: M/W/Mixed singles & doubles group stage; 1400-1730: M/W/Mixed singles & doubles group stage; 1930-2300: M/W/Mixed singles & doubles group stage

- Basketball: 1100-1515: W group phase (2 matches); 1715-1900: W group phase (1 match); 2100-2245: W group phase (1 match)

- Beach volleyball: 0900-1300: M/W preliminary phase (4 matches); 1500-1800: M/W preliminary phase (3 matches); 2000-2300: M/W preliminary phase (3 matches)

- Boxing: 1100-1310: W 60kg, M 63.5kg, M +92kg round of 32 or round of 16; 1530-1740: W 60kg, M 63.5kg, M +92kg round of 32 or round of 16; 2000-2210: W 60kg, M 63.5kg, M +92kg round of 32 or round of 16

- Canoe slalom: **1530-1830: M C1 semis, finals**

- Diving: **1100-1200: M synchro 10m platform final**

- Equestrian: **1100-1630: Eventing jumping team final, eventing jumping ind. final**

- Fencing: 0930-1650: M foil, W sabre through quarters; **1900-2310: M foil, W sabre semis, medal finals**

- Handball: 0900-1230: M preliminaries (2 matches); 1400-1730: M preliminaries (2 matches); 1900-2230: M preliminaries (2 matches)

- Hockey: 1000-1500: M pool stage (2 matches); 1030-1530: W pool stage (2 matches); 1700-2200: W pool stage (2 matches); 1730-2230

- Judo: 1000-1400: W -57kg, M -73kg elimination rounds; **1600-1900: W -57kg, M -73kg medal rounds**

- Mountain bike: **1400-1630: M cross-country final**

- Rowing: 0930-1220: M single sculls, W single sculls semis E/F, M coxless pair, W pais, M lightweight double sculls, W lightweight double sculls, M quadruple sculls, W quadruple sculls repechage, M eight, W eight heats

- Rugby sevens: 1400-1700: W pool rounds; 2000-2300: W placement matches, quarters

- Sailing: 1100-1900: M/W windsurfing, skiff

- Shooting: **0915-1305:** Mixed team 10m air pistol qualification, **M/W 10m air rifle finals**; 0900-1600: M trap qualification day 1

- Surfing: 1900-0430 (0700-1630 Tahiti time): M/W round 3

- Swimming: 1100-1300: W 400m IM, W 100m back, M 800m free heats; **2030-2230: W 400m IM, M 200m free finals**, W 100m back semis, **M 100m back, W 100m breast, W 200m free finals**

- Table tennis: 1000-1400: M/W singles round 1; 1600-1800: Mixed doubles semis; 2000-2300: M/W singles round 2

- Tennis: 1200-1700 (Court Philippe Chartrier): M/W singles; 1900-2300 (Court Philippe Chartrier): M/W singles; 1200-1900 (Court Suzanne Lenglen): M/W singles, M/W/Mixed doubles; 1200-1900 (Court Simonne Mathieu): M/W singles, M/W/Mixed doubles; 1200-1900 (outside courts): M/W singles, M/W/Mixed doubles

- Volleyball: 0900-1130: W preliminary round; 1300-1530: W

preliminary round; 1700-1930: W preliminary round; 2100-2330: W preliminary round

- Water polo: 1400-1700: W preliminary round (2 matches); 1830-2130: W preliminary round (2 matches)

Tuesday 30 July 2024 (14 gold medal events)

- Archery: 1200-1555: M/W ind. eliminations; 1745-2025: M/W ind. eliminations

- Artistic gymnastics: **1815-2030: W team final**

- Badminton: 0830-1200: M/W singles & doubles group stage; 1400-1730: M/W singles & doubles group stage; 1930-2300: M/W singles & doubles group stage

- Basketball: 1100-1515: M group phase (2 matches); 1715-1900: M group phase (1 match); 2100-2245: M group phase (1 match)

- Basketball 3X3: 1730-1930: M/W pool round (4 matches); 2100-2300: M/W pool round (4 matches)

- Beach volleyball: 0900-1300: M/W preliminary phase (4 matches); 1500-1800: M/W preliminary phase (3 matches); 2000-2300: M/W preliminary phase (3 matches)

- BMX freestyle: 1325-1630: M/W seeding round

- Boxing: 1100-1340: W 54kg, W 57kg, M 51kg, M 80kg round of 32 or round of 16; 1530-1810: W 54kg, W 57kg, M 51kg, M 80kg round of 32 or round of 16; 2000-2240: W 54kg, W 57kg, M 51kg, M 80kg round of 32 or round of 16

- Canoe slalom: 1500-1910: M K1 heats, W C1 heats

- Equestrian: 1100-1630: Dressage Grand Prix qualifier

- Fencing: 1200-1730: W épée team through semis, placement

matches; **1930-2140: W épée team medal finals**

- Football: 1500-2300: M group stage (8 matches)

- Handball: 0900-1230: W preliminaries (2 matches); 1400-1730: W preliminaries (2 matches); 1900-2230: W preliminaries (2 matches)

- Hockey: 1000-1500: M pool stage (2 matches); 1030-1530: M pool stage (2 matches); 1700-2200: M pool stage (2 matches)

- Judo: 1000-1400: W -63kg, M -81kg elimination rounds; **1600-1900: W -63kg, M -81 kg medal rounds**

- Rowing: 0930-1150: W single sculls, M single sculls quarters, W double sculls, M double sculls semis, W four, M four repechage

- Rugby sevens: **1430-2045: W placement matches, semis, medal finals**

- Sailing: 1100-1900: M/W windsurfing, skiff

- Shooting: **0930-1050: Mixed team 10m air pistol finals**; 0900-1705: W trap qualification day 1, **M trap qualification day 2 and finals**

- Surfing: **1900-0450 (0700-1650 Tahiti time): M/W quarters, semis, finals**

- Swimming: 1100-1300: W 200m fly, M 100m free, W 1500m free, W 100m free, M 200m breast, M 4x200m free relay heats; **2030-2230:** M 100m free, W 200m fly semis, **W 100m back, M 800m free finals**, W 100m free, M 200m breast semis, **M 4x200m free relay final**

- Table tennis: 1000-1200: M/W singles round 2; **1330-1600: Mixed doubles medal finals**

- Tennis: 1200-1700 (Court Philippe Chartrier): M/W singles; 1900-2300 (Court Philippe Chartrier): M/W singles; 1200-1900 (Court Suzanne Lenglen): M/W singles, M/W/Mixed doubles; 1200-1900 (Court Simonne Mathieu): M/W singles, M/W/Mixed doubles; 1200-1900 (outside courts): M/W singles, M/W/Mixed doubles

- Triathlon: **0800-1030: M ind. final**

- Volleyball: 0900-1130: M preliminary round; 1300-1530: M preliminary round; 1700-1930: M preliminary round; 2100-2330: M preliminary round

- Water polo: 1030-1330: M preliminary round (2 matches); 1500-1800: M preliminary round (2 matches); 1930-2230: M preliminary round (2 matches)

Wednesday 31 July 2024 (17 gold medal events)

- Archery: 1200-1555: M/W ind. eliminations; 1745-2025: M/W ind. eliminations

- Artistic gymnastics: **1730-2015: M ind. all-around final**

- Badminton: 0830-1200: M/W singles group stage; 1400-1730: M/W singles group stage; 1930-2300: M/W singles group play stage, Mixed doubles quarters

- Basketball: 1100-1515: M/W group phase (2 matches); 1715-1900: M/W group phase (1 match); 2100-2245: M/W group phase (1 match)

- Basketball 3X3: 1730-1930: M/W pool round (4 matches); 2100-2300: M/W pool round (4 matches)

- Beach volleyball: 0900-1300: M/W preliminary phase (4 matches); 1500-1800: M/W preliminary phase (3 matches); 2000-2300: M/W preliminary phase (3 matches)

- BMX freestyle: **1310-1630: M/W final**

- Boxing: 1100-1325: W 60kg quarters, W 66kg, M 57kg, M 71kg round of 32 or round of 16; 1530-1810: W 60kg quarters, W 66kg, M 57kg, M 71kg round of 32 or round of 16; 2000-2225: W 60kg quarters, W 66kg, M 57kg, M 71kg round of 32 or round of 16

- Canoe slalom: **1530-1830: W C1 semis, finals**

- Diving: **1100-1200: W synchro 10m platform final**

- Equestrian: 1000-1530: Dressage Grand Prix qualifier

- Fencing: 1200-1730: M sabre team through semis, placement matches; **1930-2140: M sabre team medal finals**

- Football: 1700-2300: W group stage (6 matches)

- Handball: 0900-1230: M preliminaries (2 matches); 1400-1730: M preliminaries (2 matches); 1900-2230: M preliminaries (2 matches)

- Hockey: 1000-1500: W pool stage (2 matches); 1030-1530: W pool stage (2 matches); 1700-2200: M/W pool stage (2 matches); 1730-2230: M/W pool stage (2 matches)

- Judo: 1000-1400: W -70kg, M -90kg elimination rounds; **1600-1900: W -70kg, M -90kg medal rounds**

- Rowing: **0930-1310:** M lightweight double sculls, W lightweight double sculls final C, M single sculls, W single sculls semis C/D, M coxless pair, W coxless pair, M lightweight double sculls, W lightweight double sculls semis, **M quadruple sculls, W quadruple sculls final B and medal final**

- Sailing: 1100-1900: M/W skiff

- Shooting: 0900-1030: M 50m rifle 3 pos. qualification; **0900-1705: W trap qualification day 2 and finals**

- Surfing: Reserve day

- Swimming: 1100-1300: W 200m breast, M 200m back, W 200m fly heats; **2030-2230: W 100m free, M 200m fly, M 200m breast, W 1500m free finals**, M 200m back, W 200m breast, M 200m fly semis, **M 100m free final**

- Table tennis: 1000-1300: M/W singles round 2; 1500-1800: M/W singles round 3; 2000-2300: M/W singles round 3

- Tennis: 1200-1700 (Court Philippe Chartrier): M/W singles; 1900-2300 (Court Philippe Chartrier): M/W singles; 1200-1900 (Court Suzanne Lenglen): M/W singles, M/W/Mixed doubles; 1200-1900 (Court Simonne Mathieu): M/W singles, M/W/Mixed doubles; 1200-1900 (outside courts): M singles, W/Mixed doubles

- Triathlon: **0800-1040: W ind. final**

- Volleyball: 0900-1130: M preliminary round; 1300-1530: M preliminary round; 1700-1930: W preliminary round; 2100-2330: W preliminary round

- Water polo: 1400-1700: W preliminary round (2 matches); 1830-2130: W preliminary round (2 matches)

Thursday 1 August 2024 (18 gold medal events)

- Archery: 0930-1325: M/W ind. eliminations; 1530-1925: M/W ind. eliminations

- Artistic gymnastics: **1815-2025: W ind. all-around final**

- Athletics (track and field): **0730-0905: M 20km race walk final; 0920-1105: W 20km race walk final**

- Badminton: 0830-1100: M singles round of 16, W doubles quarters; 1300-1630: M doubles quarters, M singles round of 16; 1830-2200: W singles round of 16, Mixed doubles semis

- Basketball: 1100-1515: W group phase (2 matches); 1715-1900: W group phase (1 match); 2100-2245: W group phase (1 match)

- Basketball 3X3: 0900-1100: M/W pool round (4 matches); 1230-1430: M/W pool round (4 matches); 1800-2000: M/W pool round (4 matches); 2130-2330: M/W pool round (4 matches)

- Beach volleyball: 0900-1300: M/W preliminary phase (4 matches); 1500-1800: M/W preliminary phase (3 matches); 2000-2300: M/W preliminary phase (3 matches)

- BMX racing: 2000-2220: M/W quarters and last-chance runs

- Boxing: 1100-1325: W 50kg, W 75kg round of 32 or round of 16, W 54kg, M 63.5kg, M 92kg quarters; 1530-1810: W 50kg, W 75kg round of 32 or round of 16, W 54kg, M 63.5kg, M 92kg quarters; 2000-2225: W 50kg, W 75kg round of 32 or round of 16, W 54kg, M 63.5kg, M 92kg quarters

- Canoe slalom: **1530-1835: M K1 semis, finals**

- Equestrian: 1100-1400: Jumping team qualifier

- Fencing: 1000-1710: W foil team through semis, placement matches; **1910-2200: W foil team medal finals**

- Golf: 0900-1800: M golf round 1

- Handball: 0900-1230: W preliminaries (2 matches); 1400-1730: W preliminaries (2 matches); 1900-2230: W preliminaries (2 matches)

- Hockey: 1000-1500: M pool stage (2 matches); 1030-1530: M pool stage (2 matches); 1700-2200: W pool stage (2 matches); 1730-2230

- Judo: 1000-1400: W -78kg, M -100kg elimination rounds; **1600-1900: W -78kg, M -100kg medal rounds**

- Rowing: **0930-1240:** W single sculls, M single sculls semis, W eight, M eight repechage, W double sculls, M double sculls, W coxless four, M coxless four final B, **W double sculls, M double sculls, W coxless four, M coxless four medal final**

- Sailing: **1100-1900: M/W skiff medal races**, M/W windsurfing, dinghy

- Shooting: **0930-1050: M 50m rifle 3 pos. finals**; 1200-1330: W 50m rifle 3 pos. qualification

- Surfing: Reserve day

- Swimming: 1100-1300: W 200m back, M 50m free, M 200m IM, W 4x200m free relay heats; **2030-2230: W 200m fly, M 200m back finals**, W 200m back semis, **W 200m breast final**, M 200m IM, M 50m free semis, **W 4x200m free relay final**

- Table tennis: 1000-1300: M/W singles quarters; 1500-1800: M/W singles quarters; 2000-2300: M/W singles quarters

- Tennis: 1200-1700 (Court Philippe Chartrier): M singles quarters, W singles semis; 1900-2300 (Court Philippe Chartrier): M singles quarters, W singles semis; 1200-1900 (Court Suzanne Lenglen):

M singles quarters, W/Mixed doubles semis; 1200-1900 (Court Simonne Mathieu): W/Mixed doubles semis

- Volleyball: 0900-1130: W preliminary round; 1300-1530: W preliminary round; 1700-1930: W preliminary round; 2100-2330: W preliminary round

- Water polo: 1030-1330: M preliminary round (2 matches); 1500-1800: M preliminary round (2 matches); 1930-2230: M preliminary round (2 matches)

Friday 2 August 2024 (23 gold medal events)

- Archery: 0930-1205: Mixed team eliminations; **1415-1725: Mixed team medal rounds**

- Athletics (track and field): 1005: M decathlon 100m; 1010: M hammer throw qualification A; 1015: W high jump qualification; 1035: W 100m preliminary round; 1055: M decathlon long jump; 1105: M 1500m round 1; 1135: M hammer throw qualification B; 1150: W 100m round 1; 1215: M decathlon shot put; 1800: M decathlon high jump; 1810: W 5000m round 1; 1815: W triple jump qualification; 1855: W discus throw qualification A; 1910: Mixed 4x400m relay round 1; 1945: W 800m round 1; 2010: M shot put qualification; 2020: W discus throw qualification B; 2050: M decathlon 400m; **2120: M 10,000m final**

- Badminton: 0830-1300: M/W doubles semis; **1500-2230: M singles quarters, Mixed doubles medal matches**

- Basketball: 1100-1515: M group phase (2 matches); 1715-1900: M group phase (1 match); 2100-2245: M group phase (1 match)

- Basketball 3X3: 0900-1100: M/W pool round (4 matches); 1230-1430: M/W pool round (4 matches); 1730-1930: M/W pool round (4 matches); 2100-2300: M/W pool round (4 matches)

- Beach volleyball: 0900-1300: M/W preliminary phase (4 matches); 1500-1800: M/W preliminary phase (3 matches); 2000-2300: M/W preliminary phase (3 matches)

- BMX racing: **2000-2230: M/W semis and finals**

- Boxing: 1530-1810: W 57kg round of 32 or round of 16, M 51kg, M 80kg, M +92kg quarters; 2000-2240: W 57kg round of 32 or round of 16, M 51kg, M 80kg, M +92kg quarters

- Diving: **1100-1200: M synchro 3m springboard final**

- Equestrian: **1400-1630: Jumping team final**

- Fencing: 1200-1730: M épée team through semis, placement matches; **1930-2140: M épée team medal finals**

- Football: 1500-0000: M quarters (4 matches)

- Golf: 0900-1800: M golf round 2

- Handball: 0900-1230: M preliminaries (2 matches); 1400-1730: M preliminaries (2 matches); 1900-2230: M preliminaries (2 matches)

- Hockey: 1000-1500: W pool stage (2 matches); 1030-1530: M pool stage (2 matches); 1700-2200: M pool stage (2 matches); 1730-2230

- Judo: 1000-1400: W +78kg, M +100kg elimination rounds; **1600-1900: W +78kg, M +100kg medal rounds**

- Rowing: **0930-1250:** M single sculls, W single sculls finals F/E/D, M coxless pair, W coxless pair, M lightweight double sculls, W lightweight double sculls final B, **M coxless pair, W coxless pair, M lighweight double sculls, W lightweight double sculls medal final**

- Sailing: **1100-1900: M/W windsurfing medal series**, M/W/Mixed dinghy

- Shooting: 0900-1400: W 25m pistol qualification; **0930-1050: W 50m rifle 3 pos. finals**; 0900-1430: M skeet qualification day 1

- Surfing: Reserve day

- Swimming: 1100-1300: M 100m fly, W 200m IM, W 800m free, Mixed 4x100m medley relay heats; **2030-2230: M 50m free, W 200m back, M 200m IM finals**, M 100m fly, W 200m IM semis

- Table tennis: 1000-1200: M/W singles semis; 1330-1530: M/W singles semis

- Tennis: **1200-1700** (Court Philippe Chartrier): M singles semis, **W singles bronze medal final**; **1900-2330** (Court Philippe Chartrier): M singles semis, **Mixed doubles gold medal final**; **1200-1700** (Court Suzanne Lenglen): **M/Mixed doubles bronze medal final**

- Trampoline gymnastics: **1200-1430: W final; 1800-2030: M final**

- Volleyball: 0900-1130: M preliminary round; 1300-1530: M preliminary round; 1700-1930: M preliminary round; 2100-2330: M preliminary round

- Water polo: 1400-1700: W preliminary round (2 matches); 1830-2130: W preliminary round (2 matches)

Saturday 3 August 2024 (28 gold medal events)

- Archery: 0930-1115: W ind. eliminations; **1300-1520: W ind. medal rounds**

- Artistic gymnastics: **1500-1800: Apparatus finals**

- Athletics (track and field): 1005: M decathlon 110m hurdles; 1010: M pole vault qualification; 1035: M 100m preliminary round; 1055: M decathlon discus throw A; 1110: W 800m repechage; 1145: M 100m round 1; 1200: M decathlon discus throw B; 1340: M decathlon pole vault; 1910: M decathlon javelin throw A; 1915: M 1500m repechage; **1935: M shot put final**; 1950: W 100m semis; 2010: M decathlon javelin throw B; **2020: W triple jump final**; **2055: Mixed 4x400m relay final**; **2120: W 100m final**; **2145: M decathlon 1500m final**

- Badminton: 0830-1300: W singles quarters; **1500-1730: W doubles medal matches**

- Basketball: 1100-1515: M/W group phase (2 matches); 1715-1900: M/W group phase (1 match); 2100-2245: M/W group phase (1 match)

- Basketball 3X3: 1730-1930: W Pool round (4 matches); 2130-2230: W Play-in round (2 matches)

- Beach volleyball: 0900-1300: M/W preliminary phase (4 matches); 1600-1900: M/W preliminary phase or lucky loser round (3 matches); 2100-0000: M/W lucky loser round (3 matches)

- Boxing: **1530-1755: W 50kg, W 66kg, M 57kg, M 71kg quarters,**

W 60kg semis; 2000-2225: W 50kg, W 66kg, M 57kg, M 71kg quarters, **W 60kg semis**

- Canoe slalom: 1530-1915: M/W kayak cross single time trials and repechage rounds

- Equestrian: **1000-1630: Dressage Grand Prix Special team final**

- Fencing: 1130-1700: W sabre team through semis, placement matches; **1900-2110: W sabre team medal finals**

- Football: 1500-0000: W quarters (4 matches)

- Golf: 0900-1800: M golf round 3

- Handball: 0900-1230: W preliminaries (2 matches); 1400-1730: W preliminaries (2 matches); 1900-2230: W preliminaries (2 matches)

- Hockey: 1000-1500: W pool stage (2 matches); 1030-1530: W pool stage (2 matches); 1700-2200: W pool stage (2 matches)

- Judo: 0800-1400: Mixed team elimination rounds, repechage, semis; **1600-1900: Mixed team medal rounds**

- Road cycling: **1100-1815: M road race**

- Rowing: **0930-1140: W single sculls, M single sculls finals C/B and medal final, W eight, M eight medal final**

- Sailing: 1100-1900: M/W/Mixed dinghy, Mixed multihull

- Shooting: **0930-1050: W 25m pistol finals**; 0900-1705: W skeet qualification day 1, **M skeet qualification day 2 and finals**

- Surfing: Reserve day

- Swimming: 1100-1300: W 50m free, M 1500m free, M 4x100m medley relay, W 4x100m medley relay heats; **2030-2230: M 100m fly final**, W 50m free semis, **W 200m IM, W 800m free, Mixed 4x100m medley relay finals**

- Table tennis: **1330-1600: W singles medal finals**

- Tennis: **1200-1900** (Court Philippe Chartrier): **M singles bronze medal final, W singles, M doubles gold medal finals**

- Volleyball: 0900-1130: W preliminary round; 1300-1530: W preliminary round; 1700-1930: M preliminary round; 2100-2330: M preliminary round

- Water polo: 1030-1330: M preliminary round (2 matches); 1500-1800: M preliminary round (2 matches); 1930-2230: M preliminary round (2 matches)

Sunday 4 August 2024 (20 gold medal events)

- Archery: 0930-1115: M ind. eliminations; 1300-1520: M ind. medal rounds

- Artistic gymnastics: 1500-1725: Apparatus finals

- Athletics (track and field): 1005: W 3000m steeplechase round 1; 1020: W hammer throw qualification A; 1055: W 200m round 1; 1100: M long jump qualification; 1145: W hammer throw qualification B; 1150: M 110m hurdles round 1; 1235: W 400m hurdles round 1; 1905: M 400m round 1; 1950: W high jump final; 2000: M 100m semis; 2030: M hammer throw final; 2035: W 800m semis; 2110: M 1500m semis; 2150: M 100m final

- Badminton: 0830-1300: M/W singles semis; 1500-1730: M doubles medal matches

- Basketball: 1100-1515: W group phase (2 matches); 1715-1900: W group phase (1 match); 2100-2245: W group phase (1 match)

- Basketball 3X3: 1730-1930: M pool round (4 matches); 2130-2230: M Play-in round (2 matches)

- Beach volleyball: 0900-1100: M/W round of 16 (2 matches); 1300-1500: M/W round of 16 (2 matches); 1700-1900: M/W round of 16 (2 matches); 2100-2300: M/W round of 16 (2 matches)

- Boxing: 1100-1325: W 57kg

- Canoe slalom: 1530-1725: M/W kayak cross single heats

- Equestrian: 1000-1400: Dressage Grand Prix Freestyle ind. final

- Fencing: 1000-1710: M foil team through semis

- Golf: 0900-1830: M golf round 4 (medal final)

- Handball: 0900-1230: M preliminaries (2 matches); 1400-1730: M preliminaries (2 matches); 1900-2230: M preliminaries (2 matches)

- Hockey: 1000-1500: M quarters (2 matches); 1730-2230: M quarters (2 matches)

- Road cycling: 1400-1845: W road race

- Rowing: Reserve day

- Sailing: 1100-1900: M/W Kite

- Shooting: 0900-1700: M 25m rapid fire pistol qualification; 0930-1705: W skeet qualification day 2 and finals

- Surfing: Reserve day

- Swimming: 1830-2030: W 50m free

- Table tennis: 1330-1600: M singles medal finals

- Tennis: 1200-1900 (Court Philippe Chartrier): W doubles bronze

- Volleyball: 0900-1130: W preliminary round; 1300-1530: W preliminary round; 1700-1930: W preliminary round; 2100-2330: W preliminary round

- Water polo: 1400-1700: W preliminary round (2 matches); 1830-2130: W preliminary round (2 matches)

Monday 5 August 2024 (17 gold medal events)

- Artistic gymnastics: **1200-1515: Apparatus finals**

- Artistic swimming: 1930-2100: Team technical routine

- Athletics (track and field): 1005: M 400m hurdles round 1; 1010: M discus throw qualification A; 1040: W pole vault qualification; 1050: W 400m hurdles repechage; 1120: M 400m repechage; 1135: M discus throw qualification B; 1155: W 400m round 1; 1250: W 200m repechage; **1900: M pole vault final**; 1904: M 3000m steeplechase round 1; 1955: M 200m round 1; **2035: W discus throw final**; 2045: W 200m semis; **2110: W 5000m final; 2145: W 800m final**

- Badminton: **0945-1230: W singles medal matches; 1430-1730: M singles medal matches**

- Basketball 3X3: 1730-1930: M/W semis; **2100-2320: M/W medal finals**

- Beach volleyball: 0900-1100: M/W round of 16 (2 matches); 1300-1500: M/W round of 16 (2 matches); 1700-1900: M/W round of 16 (2 matches); 2100-2300: M/W round of 16 (2 matches)

- Canoe slalom: **1530-1730: M/W kayak cross semis, finals**

- Diving: 1000-1210: W 10m platform preliminary; 1500-1700: W 10m platform semis

- Equestrian: 1400-1800: Jumping ind. qualifier

- Football: 1800-2100; 2100-0000: M semis

- Hockey: 1000-1500: W quarters (2 matches); 1730-2230: W quarters (2 matches)

- Sailing: 1100-1900: M/W Kite, M/W/Mixed dinghy, Mixed multihull

- Shooting: **0930-1050: M 25m rapid fire pistol finals; 0900-1635: Mixed team skeet qualification and finals**

- Sport climbing: 1000-1400: M boulder/lead semis (boulder), W speed qualification

- Table tennis: 1000-1300: M/W team round of 16; 1500-1800: M/W team round of 16; 2000-2300: M/W team round of 16

- Track cycling: **1700-1940:** M team sprint qualifying, M team pursuit qualifying, **W team sprint qualifying, first round, medal finals**

- Triathlon: **0800-1010: Mixed team relay final**

- Volleyball: 0900-1130: M quarters; 1300-1530: M quarters; 1700-1930: M quarters; 2100-2330: M quarters

- Water polo: 1200-1630: M preliminary round (3 matches); 1830-2300: M preliminary round (3 matches)

- Wrestling: 1500-1700: M Greco-Roman 60kg, M Greco-Roman 130kg, W freestyle 68kg round of 16, quarters; 2100-2200: M Greco-Roman 60kg, M Greco-Roman 130kg, W freestyle 68kg semis

Tuesday 6 August 2024 (15 gold medal events)

- Artistic swimming: 1930-2100: Team free routine

- Athletics (track and field): 1005: W 1500m round 1; 1020: M javelin throw qualification A; 1050: M 110m hurdles repechage; 1115: W long jump qualification; 1120: W 400m repechage; 1150: M javelin throw qualification B; 1200: M 400m hurdles repechage; 1230: M 200m repechage; 1935: M 400m semis; **1955: W hammer throw final**; 2007: W 400m hurdles semis; **2015: M long jump final**; **2050: M 1500m final**; **2110: W 3000m steeplechase final**; **2140: W 200m final**

- Basketball: 1100-1300: M quarters; 1430-1630: M quarters; 1800-2000: M quarters; 2130-2330: M quarters

- Beach volleyball: 1700-1900: M/W quarters (2 matches); 2100-2300: M/W quarters (2 matches)

- Boxing: **2130-2330: W 50kg, W 66kg, M 71kg semis, W 60kg final**

- Canoe sprint: 0930-1450: M C2 500m, M K1 1000m, M K4 500m, W C2 500m, W K1 500m, W K4 500m heats and quarters

- Diving: 1000-1200: M 3m springboard preliminary; **1500-1700: W 10m platform final**

- Equestrian: **1000-1230: Jumping ind. final**

- Football: 1800-2100; 2100-0000: W semis

- Handball: 0930-1130: W quarters; 1330-1530: W quarters;

1730-1930: W quarters; 2130-2330: W quarters

- Hockey: 1400-1600: M semis; 1900-2100: M semis

- Sailing: **1100-1900: M/W dinghy medal races**, M/W Kite, Mixed dinghy, Mixed multihull

- Skateboard: 1230-1600: W park preliminaries; **1730-1900: W park medal final**

- Sport climbing: 1000-1400: W boulder/lead semis (boulder), M speed qualification

- Table tennis: 1000-1300: M/W team round of 16; 1500-1800: M/W team quarters; 2000-2300: M/W team quarters

- Track cycling: **1730-1955: M team sprint first round, medal finals**, M team pursuit first round, W team pursuit qualifying

- Volleyball: 0900-1130: W quarters; 1300-1530: W quarters; 1700-1930: W quarters; 2100-2330: W quarters

- Water polo: 1400-1700: W quarters (2 matches); 1900-2200: W quarters (2 matches)

- Wrestling: 1100-1330: M Greco-Roman 60kg, M Greco-Roman 130kg, W freestyle 68kg repechage, M Greco-Roman 77kg, M Greco-Roman 97kg, W freestyle 50kg round of 16 and quarters; **1815-2200:** M Greco-Roman 77kg, M Greco-Roman 97kg, W freestyle 50kg semis, **M Greco-Roman 60kg, M Greco-Roman 130kg, W freestyle 68kg medal finals**

Wednesday 7 August 2024 (21 gold medal events)

- Artistic swimming: **1930-2115: Team acrobatic routine (medal final)**

- Athletics (track and field): **0730-1045: Marathon race walk mixed relay final**; 1005: M high jump qualification; 1015: W 100m hurdles round 1; 1025: W javelin throw qualification A; 1100: M 5000m round 1; 1145: M 800m round 1; 1150: W javelin throw qualification B; 1235: W 1500m repechage; **1900: W pole vault final**; 1905: M 110m hurdles semis; 1915: M triple jump qualification; 1935: M 400m hurdles semis; 2002: M 200m semis; **2025: M discus throw final;** 2045: W 400m semis; **2120: M 400m final; 2140: M 3000m steeplechase final**

- Basketball: 1100-1300: W quarters; 1430-1630: W quarters; 1800-2000: W quarters; 2130-2330: W quarters

- Beach volleyball: 1700-1900: M/W quarters (2 matches); 2100-2300: M/W quarters (2 matches)

- Boxing: **2130-2330: W 57kg, M +92kg semis, M 63.5kg, M 80kg final**

- Canoe sprint: 0930-1510: M C1 1000m, M K2 500m, W C1 200m, W K2 500m heats and quarters

- Diving: 1000-1200: M 3m springboard semis; 1500-1700: W 3m springboard preliminary

- Golf: 0900-1800: W golf round 1

- Handball: 0930-1130: M quarters; 1330-1530: M quarters;

1730-1930: M quarters; 2130-2330: M quarters

- Hockey: 1400-1600: W semis; 1900-2100: W semis

- Sailing: **1100-1900: Mixed dinghy, Mixed multihull medal races**, M/W Kite

- Skateboard: 1230-1600: M park preliminaries; **1730-1900: M park medal final**

- Sport climbing: **1000-1315:** M boulder/lead semis (lead), **W speed medal finals**

- Table tennis: 1000-1300: M/W team quarters; 1500-1800: M/W team quarters; 2000-2300: M team semis

- Taekwondo: 0900-1230: M 58kg, W 49kg qualification rounds; 1430-1730: M 58kg, W 49kg quarters, semis; **1930-2300: M 58kg, W 49kg repechage rounds and medal finals**

- Track cycling: 1245-1530: M sprint qualifying, early rounds, repechage rounds, W keirin first round, repechage, W team pursuit first round; **1730-1950:** M sprint early rounds, repechage rounds, **M team pursuit medal finals, W team pursuit medal finals**

- Volleyball: 1600-1830: M semis; 2000-2230: M semis

- Water polo: 1400-1700: M quarters (2 matches); 1900-2200: M quarters (2 matches)

- Weightlifting: **1500-1730: Men's 61kg final; 1930-2200: W 49kg final**

- Wrestling: 1100-1330: M Greco-Roman 77kg, M Greco-Roman 97kg, W freestyle 50kg repechage, M Greco-Roman 67kg, M Greco-Roman 87kg, W freestyle 53kg round of 16 and quarters; **1815-2200:** M Greco-Roman 67kg, M Greco-Roman 87kg, W freestyle 53kg semis, **M Greco-Roman 77kg, M Greco-Roman 97kg, W freestyle 50kg medal finals**

Thursday 8 August 2024 (26 gold medal events)

- Athletics (track and field): 1005: W heptathlon 100m hurdles; 1025: W shot put qualification; 1035: W 100m hurdles repechage; 1105: W heptathlon high jump; 1110: W 4x100m relay round 1; 1135: M 4x100m relay round 1; 1200: M 800m repechage; 1935: W heptathlon shot put; 1935: W 1500m semis; **2000: W long jump final; 2025: M javelin throw final; 2030: M 200m final**; 2055: W heptathlon 200m; **2125: W 400m hurdles final; 2145: M 110m hurdles final**

- Basketball: 1730-1930: M semis; 2100-2300: M semis

- Beach volleyball: 1700-1900: M/W semis (2 matches); 2100-2300: M/W semis (2 matches)

- Boxing: **2130-2330: W 75kg, M 57kg semis, W 54kg, M 51kg final**

- Canoe sprint: **1030-1430: M C2 500m, M K4 500m, W C2 500m, W K4 500m semis and finals**

- Diving: 1000-1200: W 3m springboard semis; **1500-1700: M 3m springboard final**

- Football: **1700-2000: M bronze-medal game**

- Golf: 0900-1800: W golf round 2

- Handball: 1630-1830: W semis; 2130-2330: W semis

- Hockey: **1400-1600: M bronze-medal game; 1900-2130: M gold-medal game**

- Modern pentathlon: 1100-1730: M/W fencing ranking round

- Rhythmic gymnastics: 1000-1300: Ind. All-around qualification; 1500-1800: Ind. all-around qualification

- Sailing: **1100-1900: M/W Kite medal series**

- Sport climbing: **1000-1315:** W boulder/lead semis (lead), **M speed medal finals**

- Swimming: **0730-1030: W 10km marathon final**

- Table tennis: 1000-1300: M team semis; 1500-1800: W team semis; 2000-2300: W team semis

- **Taekwondo:** 0900-1230: M 68kg, W 57kg qualification rounds; 1430-1730: M 68kg, W 57kg quarters, semis; **1930-2300: M 68kg, W 57kg repechage rounds and medal finals**

- Track cycling: **1700-1955:** M sprint quarters, classification races, **M omnium (medal final), W keirin quarters, semis, medal final**

- Volleyball: 1600-1830: W semis; 2000-2230: W semis

- Water polo: 1300-1600: W classification matches & semis (2 matches); 1800-2100: W classification matches & semis (2 matches)

- Weightlifting: **1500-1730: W 59kg final; 1930-2200: M 73kg final**

- Wrestling: 1100-1330: M Greco-Roman 67kg, M Greco-Roman 87kg, W freestyle 53kg repechage, M freestyle 57kg, M freestyle 86kg, W freestyle 57kg round of 16 and quarters; **1815-2200:** M freestyle 57kg, M freestyle 86kg, W freestyle 57kg semis, **M Greco-Roman 67kg, M Greco-Roman 87kg, W freestyle 53kg medal finals**

Friday 9 August 2024 (33 gold medal events)

- Artistic swimming: 1930-2130: Duet technical routine

- Athletics (track and field): 1005: W heptathlon long jump; 1040: W 4x400m relay round 1; 1105: M 4x400m relay round 1; 1120: W heptathlon javelin throw A; 1130: M 800m semis; 1205: W 100m hurdles semis; 1230: W heptathlon javelin throw B; **1930: W 4x100m relay final; 1940: W shot put final; 1945: M 4x100m relay final; 2000: W 400m final; 2010: M triple jump final; 2015: W heptathlon 800m final; 2055: W 10,000m final; 2145: M 400m hurdles final**

- Basketball: 1730-1930: W semis; 2100-2300: W semis

- Beach volleyball: **2100-0000: M or W medal finals (2 matches)**

- Boxing: **2130-2330: W 50kg, W 66kg, M 71kg, M 92kg final**

- Breaking: 1600-1800: W ind. qualifying; **2000-2200: W ind. final**

- Canoe sprint: **1030-1440: M K2 500m, W C1 200m, W K2 500m semis and finals**

- Diving: 1000-1200: M 10m platform preliminary; **1500-1700: W 3m springboard final**

- Football: **1500-1800: W bronze-medal game; 1800-2130: M gold-medal game**

- Golf: 0900-1800: W golf round 3

- Handball: 1630-1830: M semis; 2130-2330: M semis

- Hockey: **1400-1600: W bronze-medal game; 2000-2230: W gold-medal game**

- Modern pentathlon: 13:00 – 19:00: M semi-final 1 and semi-final 2

- Rhythmic gymnastics: 1000-1230: Group all-around qualification; **1430-1700: Ind. all-around final**

- Sport climbing: **1000-1320: M boulder/lead medal final**

- Swimming: **0730-1030: M 10km marathon final**

- Table tennis: **1000-1300: M team bronze medal final; 1500-1830: M team gold medal final**

- Taekwondo: 0900-1230: M 80kg, W 67kg qualification rounds; 1430-1730: M 80kg, W 67kg quarters, semis; **1930-2300: M 80kg, W 67kg repechage rounds and medal finals**

- Track cycling: 1400-1545: M sprint semis, W sprint qualifying, early rounds, repechage rounds; **1800-1955: M sprint medal finals, W Madison final**, W sprint early rounds, repechage rounds

- Volleyball: **1600-1830: M bronze-medal game**

- Water polo: 1300-1600: M classification matches & semis (2 matches); 1800-2100: M classification matches & semis (2 matches)

- Weightlifting: **1500-1730: M 89kg final; 1930-2200: W 71kg final**

- Wrestling: 1100-1330: M freestyle 57kg, M freestyle 86kg, W freestyle 57kg repechage, M freestyle 74kg, M freestyle 125kg, W freestyle 62kg round of 16 and quarters; **1815-2200:** M freestyle 74kg, M freestyle 125kg, W freestyle 62kg semis, **M freestyle 57kg, M freestyle 86kg, W freestyle 57kg medal finals**

Saturday 10 August 2024 (39 gold medal events)

- Artistic swimming: **1930-2200: Duet free routine (medal final)**

- Athletics (track and field): **0800-1100: M marathon final; 1910: M high jump final; 1925: M 800m final; 1940: W javelin throw final; 1945: W 100m hurdles final; 2000: M 5000m final; 2025: W 1500m final; 2112: M 4x400m relay final; 2122: W 4x400m relay final**

- Basketball: **1100-1300: M bronze-medal game; 2130-0000: M gold-medal game**

- Beach volleyball: **2100-0000: M or W medal finals (2 matches)**

- Boxing: **2130-2330: W 57kg, W 75kg, M 57kg, M +92kg final**

- Breaking: 1600-1800: M ind. qualifying; **2000-2200: M ind. final**

- Canoe sprint: **1030-1420: M C1 1000m, M K1 1000m, W K1 500m semis and finals**

- Diving: 1000-1200: M 10m platform semis; **1500-1700: M 10m platform final**

- Football: **1700-2030: W gold-medal game**

- Golf: **0900-1830: W golf round 4 (medal final)**

- Handball: **1000-1200: W bronze-medal game; 1500-1730: W gold-medal game**

- Modern pentathlon: 09:30 – 15:30: W semi-final 1 and semi-final

2; **17:30 – 20:00: M final**

- Rhythmic gymnastics: **1400-1545: Group all-around final**

- Sport climbing: **1000-1320: W boulder/lead medal final**

- Table tennis: **1000-1300: W team bronze medal final; 1500-1830: W team gold medal final**

- Taekwondo: 0900-1230: M +80kg, W +67kg qualification rounds; 1430-1730: M +80kg, W +67kg quarters, semis; **1930-2300: M +80kg, W +67kg repechage rounds and medal finals**

- Track cycling: **1700-1950:** M keirin first round, repechage, **M Madison final**, W sprint quarters, classification races

- Volleyball: **1300-1545: M gold-medal game; 1715-1945: W bronze-medal game**

- Water polo: **0900-1200: W bronze-medal game; 1400-2100:** W/M classification matches, **W gold-medal game**

- Weightlifting: **1130-1400: M 102kg final; 1600-1830: W 81kg final; 2030-2300: M +102kg final**

- Wrestling: 1100-1330: M freestyle 74kg, M freestyle 125kg, W freestyle 62kg repechage, M freestyle 65kg, M freestyle 97kg, W freestyle 76kg round of 16 and quarters; **1815-2200:** M freestyle 65kg, M freestyle 97kg, W freestyle 76kg semis, **M freestyle 74kg, M freestyle 125kg, W freestyle 62kg medal finals**

Sunday 11 August 2024 (13 gold medal events) and closing ceremony

- Athletics (track and field): **0800-1115: W marathon final**

- Basketball: **1130-1330: W bronze-medal game; 1530-1800: W gold-medal game**

- Handball: **0900-1100: M bronze-medal game; 1330-1600: M gold-medal game**

- Modern pentathlon: **1100-1330: W final**

- Track cycling: **1100-1415: M keirin quarters, semis, medal finals, W sprint semis, medal finals, W omnium (medal final)**

- Volleyball: **1300-1545: W gold-medal game**

- Water polo: **0900-1200: M bronze-medal game; 1400-1550: M gold-medal game**

- Weightlifting: **1130-1400: W +81kg final**

- Wrestling: **1100-1430: M freestyle 65kg, M freestyle 97kg, W freestyle 76kg repechage and medal finals**

- Closing Ceremony

TOP 20 TOKYO OLYMPICS (2020 / 21) FINAL MEDALS LIST

Rank	Country	Gold	Silver	Bronze	Total
1	United States	39	41	33	113
2	China	38	32	18	88
3	Japan	27	14	17	58
4	Great Britain	22	21	22	65
5	ROC	20	28	23	71
6	Australia	17	7	22	46
7	Netherlands	10	12	14	36
8	France	10	12	11	33
9	Germany	10	11	16	37
10	Italy	10	10	20	40
11	Canada	7	6	11	24
12	Brazil	7	6	8	21
13	New Zealand	7	6	7	20
14	Cuba	7	3	5	15
15	Hungary	6	7	7	20
16	South Korea	6	4	10	20
17	Poland	4	5	5	14
18	Czech Republic	4	4	3	11
19	Kenya	4	4	2	10
20	Norway	4	2	2	8

A FEW PARISIAN "DO'S" AND "DON'TS"

International law insists that a pilgrimage to Paris must be part of everyone's life journey, and rest assured, you won't regret it. However, here's a spoiler alert – you won't be alone. The city boasts the title of the second most visited in Europe, trailing behind our old friend, London. To ensure your visit is as smooth as a well-aged Pinot Noir, follow our simple rules.

DO: Take Your Time...

Begin by relaxing. Paris undoubtedly offers an abundance of sights and activities, but a rushed approach is a surefire way to guarantee an unpleasant experience. Paris thrives on café culture and people-watching. Seize a table outdoors, order wine in broad daylight, and observe the world around you.

DON'T: Make it Easy for Pickpockets...

Tourists and pickpockets often go hand in hand, much like wolves and a flock. Wherever there are tourists, there are pickpockets. Stay vigilant. Utilize the safe in your hotel room, and avoid wandering around Paris with all your valuables on display. Gentlemen, secure your wallet in your front pocket and fasten an elastic band around it to detect any lift attempts.

DO: Learn Some French Phrases...

Basic pleasantries such as hello, goodbye, please, and thanks (Bonjour, Au Revoir, S'il Vous Plait, Merci) are essential. Additionally, equip yourself with more practical phrases like, "Can you point me in the direction of the closest bottle of wine?" (Montre-moi la bouteille de vin la plus proche?) Brush up on your French and have these phrases ready for a more immersive experience.

DON'T: Believe the Rumours...

Despite Parisians battling the stereotype of being rude, most interactions are pleasant if you begin with politeness. Dispel the preconceived notions and embrace each encounter positively.

DO: Go to the Catacombs...

Venture underground to the Catacombs, an ossuary beneath the city crafted from an old quarry. This eerie labyrinth of remains, totaling six million people, originated as a solution to the overflowing cemeteries of the

18th century. It might sound macabre, and it is, but this experience will linger in your memory forever.

DON'T: Rely on Credit Cards...

Most European cities, including Paris, may not be entirely up-to-date with electronic payments. Ensure you always have cash on hand to avoid awkward moments when attempting to pay with a credit card.

DO: Ride the Metro...

A visit to Paris isn't complete without navigating the Metro. Getting lost in its labyrinth is practically a rite of passage, so stay calm when it inevitably happens. Retain your ticket, as you may need it for your exit.

DON'T: Stop Eating...

Paris is a haven for culinary delights. Consume baguettes, cheese, snails, macaroons, and other delicacies that might be illegal elsewhere. Fear not the calories; in France, they don't count. Consider stopping only when you board your flight home.

DO: Your Research...

Paris can be overwhelming, so conduct thorough research. If queuing for five hours at the Eiffel Tower doesn't appeal to you, invest in a 'skip the line' ticket for a more enjoyable visit. Knowledge is key to enhancing your time in the city.

DON'T: Be a WIFI Hunter...

Resist the urge to aimlessly scroll through your smartphone. Put down the screen and immerse yourself in the surroundings. Download a map for offline use or, if needed, return to the art of asking strangers for directions.

VISITING PARIS

Embarking on your inaugural journey to Paris? Begin by exploring the top 10 attractions and legendary sights that define the essence of this captivating city.

These renowned sites encompass the historical, cultural, and iconic places that have become synonymous with Paris, forming the quintessential list of must-see destinations for many visitors. While it might be tempting to check them all off in a single visit, especially if your stay is brief, remember that several, like the majestic Eiffel Tower, the scenic Seine River, the monumental Arc de Triomphe, and the gleaming Sacre Coeur atop a hill, grace the Parisian skyline and are easily observable from various vantage points, whether or not you decide to explore them up close.

Consider supplementing your city exploration with a swift day trip to nearby famous locales such as the Palace of Versailles or Disneyland Paris. However, don't neglect the charm of leisurely strolls through iconic neighborhoods like the Latin Quarter or Montmartre. Bask in the tranquility of the Luxembourg Garden and embark on a serene sunset cruise along the Seine.

Devote a moment to admire the exterior of Notre Dame Cathedral, currently accessible only from the outside due to the tragic 2019 fire. Encouragingly, ongoing extensive restoration efforts aim to reopen parts of this magnificent cathedral to the public by 2024.

Ensure a visit to at least one of Paris's renowned museums to witness masterpieces firsthand. Gaze upon the Mona Lisa and Venus de Milo at the Louvre, experience Van Gogh's Starry Night at the Orsay, or immerse yourself in cutting-edge contemporary art at Pompidou.

Lastly, reserve time for exploring lesser-known and even "hidden" gems throughout Paris, even if it means foregoing some of the more popular locations listed here. You can always save those for your subsequent visit to Paris, while simultaneously cultivating a diverse collection of cherished memories.

TOP TEN THINGS TO SEE IN PARIS

1. **Eiffel Tower (Tour Eiffel) - The Premier Paris Attraction**
Towering majestically over the Parisian skyline, the Eiffel Tower stands as an iconic symbol of the city, offering breathtaking panoramic views from its three distinct levels. Many consider reaching the summit of the Eiffel Tower a top priority when exploring Paris, and for good reason.
Popular Ways to Visit the Eiffel Tower:
   - **Eiffel Tower Entry Ticket with Optional Summit Access:** Experience a hosted visit, skipping the ticket line and utilizing the expedited "groups only" security line.
   - **Eiffel Tower Stairs Tickets:** Bypass the ticket line and ascend via the stairs for a unique perspective.
   - **Eiffel Tower Guided Tour by Elevator:** Indulge in a delightful meal with views of the Paris skyline.
   While the Eiffel Tower is visible from various points in the city, the thrill of ascending to the observation platforms, watching Paris landmarks shrink below, is incomparable. Consider a professional photoshoot to immortalize your visit.
   More to Enjoy: Restaurants and a champagne bar, a seasonal ice skating rink (in some years), and captivating views through the transparent floor on the 1st level.
   Paris Discovery Tip: Given the substantial crowds, especially during peak months, secure a skip-the-line priority entrance ticket to avoid up to a 4-hour wait.

2. **Louvre Museum (Musée du Louvre) - The World's Most Visited Museum**
   The colossal Louvre Museum, welcoming over 10 million visitors annually, holds the distinction of being the world's most visited museum. Situated in the "Royal Paris" section of the 1st arrondissement, its popularity is fueled by masterpieces like the Mona Lisa, Venus de Milo, and the Winged Victory of Samothrace.
   More to Enjoy: Explore a magnificent Egyptian collection, European

paintings spanning the Middle Ages to the mid-19th century, and dazzling displays of furniture, tapestries, and ornamental objects. Descend to the basement level to view excavations of the original 12th-century fortress.

3. **Versailles Palace - France's Most Visited Royal Palace**

Boasting over 700 rooms, Versailles Palace stands among the world's largest palaces, providing a glimpse into royal life from King Louis XIV to Marie-Antoinette. The opulent Hall of Mirrors, lavishly adorned rooms, and priceless artworks make it an unforgettable day trip.

More to Enjoy: Explore magnificent gardens featuring statues, fountains, and tree-lined paths.

Paris Discovery Tip: Given Versailles' popularity, opt for skip-the-line tickets or, for an expedited experience, choose a guided tour.

4. **Latin Quarter (Quartier Latin)**

Immerse yourself in the historic charm of the Latin Quarter, initially settled by Romans in the 1st century. This Left Bank neighbourhood, with medieval traces in its narrow streets, has long been a haven for bohemians, scholars, and political activism.

More to Enjoy: Visit brasseries on Boulevard Saint Germain, explore the Pantheon, and marvel at the Lady and the Unicorn tapestries at the Cluny Museum.

5. **Seine River - Beaches, Cruises, & More**

The Seine River weaves through central Paris, delineating the Right Bank to the north and the Left Bank to the south. Île de la Cité, at its heart, houses medieval masterpieces, hidden parks, and 17th-century enclaves.

More to Enjoy: Walk along the banks, explore bouquinistes (riverside booksellers), and indulge in a Seine River cruise for unique perspectives. Experience Les Berges, the vibrant recreational area along the Left Bank.

Paris Discovery Tip: Cruise through the 15th-century Canal Saint-Martin and Canal de l'Ourcq for a novel view of the city.

6. **Notre Dame (Cathédrale Notre-Dame de Paris)**

Built during the Middle Ages on Île de la Cité, Notre Dame Cathedral showcases Gothic splendors. While interior access is limited due to the 2019 fire, ongoing restoration work promises partial reopening by December 2024.

Best Viewing Location: Left Bank of the Seine River.

7. **Montmartre and Sacré Coeur**

Formerly a separate village, Montmartre's winding lanes and picturesque hillsides retain a distinct charm. Stroll past historic cafes and cabarets, with the gleaming white Basilica of the Sacré Coeur as the centerpiece.

More to Enjoy: Explore Sacré Coeur's beautiful mosaics.

8. **Musée d'Orsay**

Housed in a former train station, Musée d'Orsay boasts an outstanding collection of Impressionist and Post-Impressionist art. While the most famous masterpieces draw crowds, the museum offers sweeping views from its rooftop terrace.

Paris Discovery Tip: Opt for a guided tour during peak times for unobstructed views.

9. **Arc de Triomphe**

The monumental Arc de Triomphe, commissioned by Napoleon in 1806, stands as a symbol of victory. Visit the observation deck for 360-degree views, and pay respects at the Tomb of the Unknown Soldier.

Best Time to View: First Sunday (car-free Sundays) of each month.

More to Enjoy: Elaborate statues and bas-relief carvings depicting Napoleon's battles.

10. **Luxembourg Garden (Jardin du Luxembourg)**

With its serene ambiance, Luxembourg Garden stands out as Paris's most popular park. The 60-acre space offers diverse areas, including tennis courts and an open-air cafe.

More to Enjoy: Pony rides and puppet theatre for children; tranquil moments by the Medici Fountain for relaxation.

Made in the USA
Coppell, TX
25 June 2024

33906236R00040